ITALIAN VEGETARIAN COOKING

IN A NUTSHELL

ITALIAN
VEGETARIAN
COOKING

A STEP-BY-STEP
GUIDE

ANNE SHEASBY

ELEMENT

SHAFTESBURY, DORSET • BOSTON, MASSACHUSETTS • MELBOURNE, VICTORIA

First published in
Great Britain in 1999 by
ELEMENT BOOKS LIMITED
Shaftesbury, Dorset SP7 8BP

Published in the USA in 1999 by
ELEMENT BOOKS INC
160 North Washington Street, Boston
MA 02114

Published in Australia in 1999 by
ELEMENT BOOKS LIMITED
and distributed by Penguin Australia Ltd
487 Maroondah Highway, Ringwood,
Victoria 3134

NOTE FROM THE PUBLISHER
Unless specified otherwise
All recipes serve four
All eggs are medium
All herbs are fresh
All spoon measurements are level

Designed and created with Element Books by
The Bridgewater Book Company Limited

ELEMENT BOOKS LIMITED
Managing Editor Miranda Spicer
Senior Commissioning Editor Caro Ness
Editor Finny Fox-Davies
Group Production Director Clare Armstrong
Production Manager Stephanie Raggett
Production Controller Claire Legg

THE BRIDGEWATER
BOOK COMPANY
Art Director Terry Jeavons
Designed by Axis Design
Project Editor Caroline Earle
Editor Jo Wells
Photography David Jordan
Home Economy Judy Williams
Picture research Caroline Thomas

Printed and bound in Portugal
by Printer Portuguesa

Library of Congress Cataloging in
Publication data available

ISBN 1 86204 481 3

The publishers wish to thank the following for
the use of pictures: Garden Picture Library
p14. The Image Bank p.8. Images
Colour Library p. 6T. Tony Stone
Images pp.6B, 19.

Contents

Italian cooking

ITALIANS ARE *great lovers of good food, which is reflected in the way they buy, prepare, and cook and in the many wonderful dishes and regional variations.*

Italy lies at the heart of the Mediterranean area. It is divided into several regions, and the cuisine of each region is affected by climate, topography, the foods that grow and local customs. So each region produces its specialties, and these add up to a rich and varied national cuisine.

Italian cookery uses an abundance of fresh vegetables, not only as accompaniments, but also as main courses, starters, and

ABOVE *Fresh ingredients are the key to Italian vegetarian cookery.*

BELOW *Olives ripen under the Mediterranean sun.*

salads. Vegetables are usually cooked in simple ways to bring out their true and natural flavors. Italians enjoy seasonal fresh fruits, ranging from oranges, cherries, peaches, and apricots to melon, fresh figs, and grapes.

The quality and freshness of food are both of great

importance to Italians. Most of the produce that is used is grown or produced locally, and market stalls are packed with fresh seasonal foods.

Olive oil is the primary fat used for cooking in Italy. It is one of the "healthier" types of fat because it is high in monounsaturated fat and low in saturated fat. Butter is more commonly used in northern Italian cooking; it is also a natural fat and often preferred.

In Italy, the most important meal of the day is usually served at lunchtime. A typical lunch may begin with a selection of *antipasti*, which are small tasty snacks, such as broiled eggplants, roasted bell peppers, and tomatoes. The first course may be a simple soup, pasta, or rice dish such as risotto, then a meat, poultry, fish, or vegetarian course served with fresh vegetables or salad. Cheese and fresh fruit usually follow, but occasionally a

AVAILABILITY

While supermarkets now stock a wide range of authentic Italian ingredients, a visit to an Italian delicatessen is well worthwhile in order to experience, enjoy, and be tempted by the wealth of delicious Italian foods and ingredients on offer.

dessert will be served. Espresso coffee often ends the meal. Wine and sparkling mineral water are served, as well as plenty of fresh local bread. After such a meal, it is not surprising that a siesta often follows!

Italian Vegetarian Cooking provides a varied and interesting insight into healthy Italian dishes that are packed full of flavor, color, and appeal, and will tempt and satisfy the tastebuds of vegetarians and non-vegetarians alike.

ABOVE **Pasta is a staple of Italian cuisine.**

LEFT **Pungent fresh Parmesan cheese.**

Healthy eating

A HEALTHY APPROACH *to eating is important for everyone, particularly as lives become more demanding and hectic.*

Following a good, well-balanced, and healthy diet by eating the correct balance and proportions of the right types of foods is simple, and provides the body with all the nutrients that it needs in order to grow and function properly. Eating a healthy diet is therefore a good basis for enjoying a happy and healthy life.

BELOW *A healthy diet means cutting out high-fat junk food.*

FAT

Reduce the amount of fat eaten, especially saturated fats found in chocolate, cakes, and pastries.

Cut down on high-fat foods such as full-fat dairy products, including whole milk, butter, margarine, cream, and cheese.

Choose low-fat or reduced-fat dairy products; cook using less fat (spray cooking oils are a good idea) or use a small amount of a poly- or mono-unsaturated oil; and broil rather than fry food.

FRUIT AND VEGETABLES

Eat at least five portions of fruit and vegetables (not including potatoes) every day. Fruit and vegetables are valuable sources of vitamins, minerals, and fiber.

APRICOTS

CARBOHYDRATE

Increase the amount of starchy carbohydrate foods, such as rice, pasta, bread, cereals, and potatoes in your diet and base meals on these foods.

Starchy foods rather than sugars and fats should be your main source of energy. They are low in fat, provide B vitamins, protein, calcium, and iron.

CIABATTA BREAD

FIBER

Increase your intake of dietary fiber. Simple ways to achieve this include eating brown or whole wheat bread, whole wheat pasta, brown rice, and wholegrain breakfast

HIGH FIBER CEREAL

cereals. When recipes call for white flour, use half white and half whole wheat flour instead.

PROTEIN

Obtain protein from low-fat dairy products, eggs, pasta, wholegrain cereals, beans, and peas. Nuts and seeds contain protein, but they are also high in fat so should be eaten in moderation.

SALT

SALT

Use salt sparingly, or use a reduced-sodium alternative to salt. Season foods with other seasonings, such as herbs and spices.

SUGAR

Add less sugar to food and cut down on high-sugar foods, such as cakes, cookies, chocolate, desserts. and pastries.

If you fancy a snack or treat, choose fresh vegetables or fruit, dried fruit (there is a wide range available), bread-sticks, pita breads, or low-fat yogurt.

SUGAR

Sources of nutrients

BASED ON PLENTY *of fresh fruit and vegetables, olive oil, and carbohydrate-rich foods, the Italian vegetarian diet is delicious and provides a wide range of essential nutrients.*

BELL PEPPERS
Bell peppers are an excellent source of vitamin C. Yellow and red bell peppers are also a good source of beta carotene (the plant form of vitamin A).

ZUCCHINI
Zucchini provide beta carotene and folate.

ONIONS
Onions are thought to help lower blood cholesterol levels, as well as reducing the risk of coronary heart disease.

ONION

GARLIC
Garlic has anti-viral, anti-bacterial, and anti-fungal properties.

GARLIC

EGGPLANTS
Eggplants provide potassium.

TOMATOES
Tomatoes are a good source of beta carotene, vitamins C and E, and potassium.

TOMATOES

MUSHROOMS
Mushrooms are good sources of potassium.

BROCCOLI
Broccoli supplies plenty of vitamin C, beta carotene, folate, iron, and potassium.

LEEKS
Leeks provide potassium and folate.

ARTICHOKES
Artichokes provide potassium and folate.

FENNEL
Fennel provides beta carotene, potassium, and folate.

FENNEL
BULB

PULSES

Pulses (dried peas, beans, and lentils) are good sources of protein and fiber, and they provide iron, potassium, magnesium, and B vitamins.

PASTA

Pasta is an excellent source of carbohydrate for energy. It also supplies protein. Whole wheat pasta is a good source of fiber.

PASTA

RICE

Rice is a rich source of starch and provides a little protein. Brown rice is useful for fiber.

POLENTA

Polenta is a good source of starch. It also supplies protein, potassium, and iron.

POLENTA

BREAD

Bread provides starch, as well as protein, fiber, iron, calcium, and B vitamins.

OLIVES

Olives contain natural

OLIVES   antioxidants, which

help to reduce the risk of cancer and heart disease, plus vitamin E and fiber. Olives are high in monounsaturated fatty acids.

PINE NUTS

Pine nuts provide protein, fiber, potassium, iron, zinc, vitamin E, and some B vitamins. They are also high in polyunsaturated fatty acids.

OLIVE OIL

Olive oil is high in monounsaturated fat and low in saturated fat. It is also a valuable

OLIVE OIL   source of vitamin E.

PARMESAN CHEESE

Parmesan cheese or Parmigiano is a good source of calcium and protein and also provides vitamin B12.

MOZZARELLA CHEESE

Mozzarella cheese provides protein,

MOZZARELLA

calcium, and some B vitamins.

RICOTTA CHEESE

Ricotta cheese is a source of protein, potassium, and calcium.

Preparing vegetables

WHATEVER VEGETABLES YOU ARE BUYING, *take care to select those that have a good color, and are firm, dry, and unwrinkled without blemishes or soft patches.*

BELL PEPPERS

Cut in half lengthwise, remove and discard the stalk, core, and seeds. Rinse and pat dry.

To peel, place (cut side down) on a rack in a broiler pan. Broil until charred and blistered (about 10 minutes). Peel when cool, with a sharp knife.

PEELED PEPPERS

ZUCCHINI

Wash or wipe the skin and slice off both ends. Slice, dice, grate coarsely, or cut into matchsticks (julienne strips).

PREPARED ZUCCHINI

ONIONS

To chop, halve lengthwise through the root, and remove the skin. Place on a chopping board, cut side down. Slice through, then again at right angles.

CHOPPED AND SLICED ONIONS

GARLIC

Avoid cloves that have green shoots. Remove the skin, and chop if required. To crush garlic without a garlic press, lay a clove on a chopping board and press down firmly with the flat of a large knife.

CRUSHED AND PEELED GARLIC

EGGPLANTS

Wash or wipe the skin, cut off the stem and trim the ends. Cut in half lengthwise, slice or dice, and use as required.

Eggplants can be salted before use to extract any bitter juices. To do this, place prepared eggplants in a colander. Sprinkle liberally with salt and leave to stand for about 15–30 minutes. Rinse thoroughly under cold water and pat dry.

DICED EGGPLANTS

TOMATOES

Wash the tomato, then quarter, slice, or chop, and use as required.

CHOPPED TOMATOES

To peel tomatoes, cut a small cross in the base of each tomato using a sharp knife. Immerse in boiling water for 20–30 seconds, then using a slotted spoon, plunge them into a bowl of cold water. Remove and peel the tomatoes – the skins should slide off easily.

MUSHROOMS

Wipe clean with a soft brush or damp cloth and trim the ends of the stalks, if necessary. Use whole or slice, dice, or chop and use as required.

SLICED MUSHROOMS

BROCCOLI

Discard any tough leaves. Cut or break into flowerets or split each stalk lengthwise 2–3 times to divide the broccoli heads. Use as required.

SLICED BROCCOLI

LEEKS

Cut off the root and top and discard the outer leaves. Slice the leeks across or lengthwise and wash thoroughly under cold running water to

SLICED LEEKS

remove any dirt and grit between the layers. Slice or chop and use as required.

FENNEL

Trim the root and stalk ends and rinse thoroughly. Quarter, slice, chop, or coarsely grate the fennel. The feathery green leaves are often removed and reserved for use as a garnish.

SPINACH

Wash the leaves gently but thoroughly in several changes of cold water to remove any dirt or grit, then shake dry. Spinach can be cooked in just the water that clings to the leaves. Tough central ribs and stalks should be removed from large leaves. Baby spinach leaves can also be used raw in salads.

BABY SPINACH

Herbs

MANY POPULAR HERBS *are native to the Mediterranean region, and fresh herbs play a pivotal role in Italian cooking, adding flavor, texture, and color to numerous dishes. Sprigs or leaves of fresh herbs or chopped herbs also make an attractive garnish.*

Herbs can be grown at home either outside in borders or tubs or on the window-sill in pots or window boxes. Fresh herbs will give maximum flavor and color. Fortunately, they are now more widely available, with most supermarkets and many market stalls offering an excellent selection.

So make the most of herbs, such as basil, when they are in season, and freeze them in small quantities to use at other times of the year. If fresh herbs are not available, use freeze-dried, ready-frozen, or bottled prepared fresh herbs instead.

The flavor of the herb comes from the essential oils stored in the leaves. The oils are released when the herb is chopped, crushed or heated.

BELOW *Even a small yard can provide plenty of fresh herbs.*

BASIL
Fresh basil is an important herb in Italian cooking and a perfect addition to tomato dishes. Basil is an important ingredient in the classic Italian sauce, pesto.

BASIL

PARSLEY
Choose flat leaf parsley, sometimes known as Italian parsley. It has a richer and more pungent flavor than the curly leaf variety. Parsley is an excellent breath freshener, particularly if chewed raw after eating garlic.

PARSLEY

OREGANO
Oregano, also known as wild marjoram, is a popular flavoring for pizzas, tomato dishes, pasta sauces, frittata, marinades, and vegetables dishes, such as stuffed vegetables.

OREGANO

ROSEMARY
Rosemary is a powerful aromatic herb which imparts a wonderful flavor to food, but it should be used in moderation. Whole sprigs can be added to dishes and removed before serving. Alternatively, the spiky green leaves can be finely chopped and added to food.

ROSEMARY

SAGE
Sage has a strong flavor and should be used sparingly. Sage is ideal in dishes containing tomatoes, garlic, or oil, in salad dressings, marinades, and vegetable soups.

SAGE

THYME
Thyme has a rich aromatic flavor which goes well in pasta sauces, pasta dishes, marinades, and vegetable casseroles.

THYME

BAY LEAVES
Bay leaves have a distinct, pungent flavor and are best used whole during cooking, then removed before serving. Whole bay leaves are used in soups, casseroles, stocks and marinades, bean stews, risottos, and vegetable dishes.

BAY LEAVES

The storecupboard

EVERY COOK NEEDS *to have a store of essential ingredients for making successful Italian dishes. Keep your pantry stocked with a range of oils, vinegars, preserves, dried pulses, pasta, and rice.*

CANNED TOMATOES

Canned or bottled peeled plum tomatoes, whole or chopped, are an essential storecupboard item in Italian cooking. They are a convenient and useful ingredient for the winter months when fresh plum tomatoes are less readily available.

SIEVED TOMATOES

This is a smooth, thick purée of sieved fresh tomatoes, usually available in jars or cartons. It is ideal for tomato sauces, pasta sauces, and soups. Once it has been opened, store the container in the refrigerator.

TOMATO PASTE

An intensely flavored concentrate or paste made from tomatoes that is widely used to boost the flavor of many Italian dishes. Tomato paste is available in tubes or cans.

SUN-DRIED TOMATOES

A tasty addition to many Italian recipes – sun-dried tomatoes are available dried or in oil in jars. Soak dried tomatoes in warm water for 20–30 minutes before using. Sun-dried tomatoes in oil are ready to use, after draining.

DRIED MUSHROOMS

Dried mushrooms such as porcini (cep) are now widely available and add a delicious flavor to sauces, stews, and risottos. Simply soak the dried mushrooms in warm water for about 20 minutes, drain, chop finely and add to the recipe.

CANNED, PEELED
PLUM TOMATOES

SUN-DRIED
TOMATOES IN OIL

READY-MADE PASTA SAUCE

TOMATO PASTE

PASTA

Fresh or dried, filled or plain, pasta comes in many shapes, sizes, and colors. Pasta may be made with plain or whole wheat flour and can be flavored with additions, such as tomatoes, garlic, herbs, chili, or spinach.

Fresh egg pasta has a limited shelf-life and should be stored in the refrigerator. Dried pasta keeps well in the storecupboard and has a much longer shelf-life. Names and types vary throughout the regions of Italy.

POLENTA

Polenta is made from ground cornmeal. Usually mixed with salted water or vegetable stock, it is often flavored with ingredients such as butter, chopped fresh herbs, garlic, or grated Parmesan cheese. Quick-cook or instant polenta, as well as ready-prepared blocks of cooked polenta, can also be bought.

RICE

Italian risotto rice is a short-grain rice which swells and absorbs up to five times its weight in liquid, but still retains a firm "bite." Arborio is the most widely available risotto rice.

BELOW *Sauces, dried pasta, preserves, pastes, and dried and canned vegetables are invaluable in Italian cooking. Keep your storecupboard well stocked with a wide range of these basic, but essential ingredients.*

DRIED SPAGHETTI

SIEVED TOMATOES

TROMPETTI

FUSILLI

SLICED DRIED MUSHROOMS

SUN-DRIED TOMATOES

SUN-DRIED TOMATO SAUCE FOR PASTA

POLENTA

WHOLE DRIED MUSHROOMS

DRIED PORCINI MUSHROOMS

DRIED TAGLIATELLE

OLIVES

Olives are picked when green or when black and fully ripe. Both are available whole or pitted and sold loose, in jars, or vacuum-packed.

OLIVES

OLIVE OIL

A wide selection of olive oils is available. Two or three bottles should suffice. Use single estate, cold-pressed, extra virgin olive oil for salad dressings, uncooked sauces, or drizzling over vegetables or bruschetta. Virgin olive oil is good for pesto, mayonnaise, and general cooking, but not frying; use a good quality pure oil for cooking and baking.

BALSAMIC VINEGAR

Balsamic vinegar has a rich, sweet-sour flavor. It is made from fermented grape juice, skins, and pits and is aged in wooden casks or barrels for at least four years. Use in moderation to flavor sauces or salad dressings.

PESTO

Pesto can be bought ready-made in jars or fresh in tubs and can be added to hot pasta, gnocchi, or rice for a quick, tasty supper.

PINE NUTS

Pine nuts are an important ingredient in pesto and are also used in Italian desserts.

VEGETABLE STOCK

For the best flavor, use fresh stock, but good quality vegetable stock cubes and pastes may be kept as a stand-by.

BEANS AND PULSES

Beans and pulses can be bought dried for soaking and cooking at home, or ready-cooked in cans; these should be drained and rinsed before use.

BALSAMIC VINEGAR AND OLIVE OIL

ABOVE *Traditional Italian delicatessens stock a wide range of local cheeses.*

FLOUR AND YEAST
Strong plain white flour and active dry yeast are ideal for making breads and pizzas.

SPONGE FINGERS
Sponge fingers, or *savoiardi*, are useful for making Italian desserts.

PARMESAN CHEESE
Parmesan cheese is a salty, crumbly, pale yellow, hard grana cheese. Parmigiano Reggiano is the best quality. Fresh Parmesan keeps well. It is best bought in one piece, then grated or sliced.

MOZZARELLA CHEESE
Mozzarella is a delicately flavored semisoft cheese, made from water buffalo's milk, or a mix of buffalo's and cow's milk. Store in its whey to keep moist.

MASCARPONE CHEESE
A fresh thick cream cheese with a mild, slightly sweet flavor, it is often served with fresh fruit or used to make Italian desserts.

RICOTTA CHEESE
A soft, smooth, unsalted white whey cheese with a clean, fresh and mild flavor, ricotta is made from ewe's or cow's milk. It should be eaten very fresh and is mostly used in cooking.

PLUM
TOMATOES

Plum Tomato and Lentil Soup

IF FRESH PLUM TOMATOES *are not available, use canned plum tomatoes or well-flavored standard tomatoes.*

INGREDIENTS

1 onion, chopped

1 garlic clove, crushed

1 tablespoon olive oil

2 pounds plum tomatoes, chopped

1 tablespoon tomato paste

2½ cups vegetable stock

½ teaspoon superfine sugar

1 bay leaf

salt and pepper

1½ cups cooked green or brown lentils

3 tablespoons chopped flat leaf parsley

VARIATIONS

● Use a leek in place of the onion.

● Use cooked beans, such as navy or cannellini, in place of the cooked lentils.

1 Place the onion and garlic in the oil in a large saucepan and cook, stirring occasionally, for 5 minutes, until softened.

2 Stir in the tomatoes, tomato paste, stock, sugar, bay leaf, and seasoning.

3 Bring to a boil, cover, and simmer for 30 minutes, stirring occasionally. Discard the bay leaf.

COOK'S TIP

A quick and easy way to keep fresh parsley is to place the parsley sprigs in a pitcher and snip off small pieces using a pair of kitchen scissors.

4 Cool slightly. Process in a blender or food processor. Rub through a strainer and return to the rinsed-out pan.

5 Stir in the cooked lentils and then reheat gently until piping hot.

6 Add the chopped parsley, and adjust the seasoning to taste. Serve hot with crusty Italian bread.

Broiled Vegetable Bruschetta

THE VEGETABLES *in this tasty snack or starter can be varied. Try red in place of yellow bell peppers, or eggplants instead of zucchini.*

INGREDIENTS

2 tablespoons olive oil, plus extra

2 yellow bell peppers, seeded and sliced into strips

2 zucchini, sliced diagonally

1 red onion, thinly sliced

3 plum tomatoes, thickly sliced

4 large thick slices of Italian country bread

2 garlic cloves, halved

Parmesan cheese shavings and basil, to garnish

ITALIAN COUNTRY BREAD

1 Pour the olive oil over the vegetables and toss lightly to coat thoroughly with oil.

RED BELL PEPPER

VARIATION

Use other types of fresh bread, such as French bread, crusty whole wheat bread, or granary bread.

2 Place half the vegetables in a single layer on a rack in the broiler pan. Cook under a hot broiler until slightly softened and lightly browned, turning once or twice.

3 Transfer to a plate and keep warm in a low oven. Repeat with the remaining vegetables.

4 Toast the bread until golden on both sides and lightly rub half a garlic clove over each slice.

5 Pile the broiled vegetables onto the slices of toast. Drizzle a little oil over the vegetables and garnish with Parmesan shavings and basil.

Tomato, Mozzarella, and Basil Salad

SLICES OF PLUM TOMATOES *and mozzarella, drizzled with fresh basil dressing, makes this simple, but typically Italian salad.*

INGREDIENTS

10 ounces mozzarella cheese, sliced

6 plum tomatoes, sliced

6 tablespoons olive oil

2 tablespoons white wine vinegar

2 scallions, finely chopped

2–3 tablespoons chopped basil

pinch of caster sugar

salt and pepper

basil sprigs, to garnish

TOMATO, MOZZARELLA, AND BASIL SALAD

1 Arrange alternate slices of mozzarella and tomato on a large serving plate.

2 Place the oil, vinegar, scallions, chopped basil, sugar, and seasoning in a small bowl and whisk together until thoroughly combined.

MOZZARELLA CHEESE

3 Drizzle the dressing over the mozzarella and tomatoes and serve—or cover and leave to chill for 1–2 hours before serving. Garnish with sprigs of basil.

SCALLIONS

VARIATIONS

● Use standard tomatoes if plum tomatoes are not available. Alternatively, use 3–4 beefsteak tomatoes in place of the plum tomatoes.

● Add 1–2 tsp Dijon or wholegrain mustard to the dressing, if preferred.

● Use walnut oil in place of olive oil.

Marinated Mushrooms with Artichokes

THE COMBINATION *of simple ingredients makes this a very convenient and appetizing starter.*

8 tablespoons olive oil

2 tablespoons balsamic vinegar

pinch of superfine sugar

1 garlic clove, crushed

2 tablespoons chopped flat leaf parsley

salt and pepper

*3 cups button mushrooms,
left whole or halved*

3 cups sliced crimini mushrooms

*14 ounce can artichoke hearts, drained,
and halved or quartered*

flat leaf parsley sprigs, to garnish

Serves 4–6

1 Place the olive oil, vinegar, sugar, garlic, parsley, and seasoning in a small bowl and whisk together until thoroughly combined.

PARSLEY

CRIMINI
MUSHROOMS

2 Put the mushrooms in a nonmetallic bowl and pour over the dressing.

3 Stir the mushrooms gently to coat them thoroughly.

4 Cover and marinate in the refrigerator for 4–6 hours.

5 Just before serving, stir the artichokes into the mushrooms.

6 Garnish with fresh parsley sprigs and serve with lightly toasted or fresh Italian bread.

COOK'S TIP

● Use mixed fresh exotic mushrooms in place of all or some of the button or crimini mushrooms.

● Use flavored vinegar, such as herb vinegar, in place of the balsamic vinegar.

Warm Mixed Bean Salad

THIS TEMPTING SALAD *of warm mixed beans and fresh vegetables tossed in a tasty tomato dressing can also be served cold.*

INGREDIENTS

15 ounce can cannellini beans

15 ounce can borlotti beans

1 red bell pepper, seeded and chopped

1 small onion, finely chopped

1½ cups sliced button mushrooms

8 ounces baby plum tomatoes or cherry tomatoes, halved

baby spinach leaves, to serve

FOR THE DRESSING

⅔ cup sieved tomatoes

4 tablespoons olive oil

1 tablespoon balsamic vinegar

1 garlic clove, crushed

3 tablespoons chopped flat leaf parsley

salt and pepper

Serves 4–6

VARIATIONS

● Add teaspoon wholegrain or Dijon mustard to the dressing.

● Sugar-snap peas can be used in place of the sliced button mushrooms.

Gently heat the canned beans and their liquid until the beans are piping hot, stirring occasionally.

Drain the beans and mix in a serving bowl with the bell pepper, onion, mushrooms and tomatoes.

To make the dressing, whisk all the ingredients together in a small bowl until thoroughly combined.

Pour the dressing over the bean salad and toss well. Serve on a bed of baby spinach leaves.

Baked Shallots with Oregano

SHALLOTS ARE *oven baked in olive oil and tossed in fresh oregano to create a delicious snack or meal accompaniment.*

INGREDIENTS

1 pound 9 ounces shallots, peeled

2 tablespoons olive oil

salt and pepper

2–3 tablespoons chopped oregano

oregano sprigs, to garnish

SHALLOTS

1 Put the peeled shallots in a shallow roasting pan or ovenproof dish. Add the oil and seasoning.

OREGANO

COOK'S TIP

Cover the shallots with boiling water and let stand for about 1–2 minutes before peeling to make the skin softer and easier to remove.

BAKED SHALLOTS WITH OREGANO

VARIATIONS

● Use baby onions in place of the shallots.

● Use chopped marjoram or rosemary instead of oregano.

2 Toss together to coat the shallots evenly.

3 Bake in a preheated oven at 400°F for 30–40 minutes, or until golden brown and tender, stirring once or twice. Add the oregano, toss to mix, and serve immediately, garnished with oregano sprigs.

Broiled Eggplants with Red Pesto

GOLDEN BROILED EGGPLANTS *with a delicious red pesto sauce is a quick and easy supper or lunchtime dish.*

INGREDIENTS

2 eggplants, each about 10 ounces, thinly sliced

olive oil, for brushing

basil sprigs, to garnish

FOR THE PESTO

⅓ cup basil leaves

⅓ cup flat leaf parsley

¼ cup pine nuts

1 garlic clove, crushed

6 sun-dried tomatoes in oil, drained

1 tablespoon tomato paste

6 tablespoons olive oil

⅔ cup freshly grated Parmesan cheese

salt and pepper

Serves 4-6

VARIATIONS

● Use 2 large zucchini in place of the eggplants.

● Use basil leaves in place of the parsley.

● Almonds can replace the pine nuts.

BROILED EGGPLANTS WITH RED PESTO

1 Lightly brush the eggplant slices with olive oil.

2 Place half the eggplant slices in a single layer on the rack in a broiler pan and broil them until golden. Turn and repeat for the other side.

3 Transfer the cooked slices to a plate and keep them warm in a low oven. Repeat step 2 with the remaining eggplant slices.

4 Meanwhile, make the red pesto: process the basil, parsley, pine nuts, garlic, sun-dried tomatoes, tomato paste, and oil in a blender or small food processor until smooth.

5 Add the Parmesan and seasoning and blend briefly.

6 Serve the hot eggplant slices with the red pesto spooned over or alongside. Garnish with basil sprigs.

Zucchini and Red Bell Pepper Frittata

A FRITTATA IS *a deep Italian omelet; served with salad, it makes a light and nutritious supper dish.*

INGREDIENTS

1 onion, chopped

1 garlic clove, crushed

1 red bell pepper, seeded and thinly sliced

1 zucchini, thinly sliced

1 tablespoon olive oil

6 ounces cooked potatoes, diced

6 eggs

1 tablespoon chopped mixed herbs

salt and pepper

⅓ cup freshly grated Parmesan cheese

OREGANO

1 Cook the onion, garlic, bell pepper and zucchini in the oil in a large nonstick skillet, stirring occasionally, for 5 minutes, or until softened.

VARIATIONS

● Use 1½ cups sliced mushrooms in place of the zucchini.

● A leek can replace the onion.

GARLIC PRESS

ZUCCHINI AND RED BELL PEPPER FRITTATA

2 Add the potatoes and cook, stirring occasionally, for 2 minutes.

3 Beat the eggs with the herbs and seasoning.

5 Sprinkle with the cheese and cook under a medium broiler until the top is lightly set and golden brown. Serve warm or cold cut into wedges, with a side salad.

4 Pour the egg mixture evenly over the vegetables in the skillet and cook over a medium heat until the eggs are beginning to set and the frittata is golden brown underneath.

Red Onion Pizza

NOW THAT *stone-baked pizza bases are easily available ready-made, it is simple to make your own pizzas.*

INGREDIENTS

1 tablespoon olive oil

2 red onions, thinly sliced

1 garlic clove, thinly sliced

8 ounce can chopped
tomatoes, drained

1 tablespoon tomato paste

2 teaspoons chopped rosemary

salt and pepper

7 ounces mozzarella cheese, sliced

⅓ cup pitted black olives

1 ready-made stone-baked pizza base

COOK'S TIP

Sprinkle the hot pizza with freshly grated Parmesan cheese just before serving.

ROSEMARY

1 To make the topping, fry the onions and garlic in the oil, stirring occasionally, for 10–15 minutes.

2 Place the pizza base on a lightly greased cookie sheet. Mix together the tomatoes, tomato paste, rosemary, and seasoning and spread over the pizza base. Spoon on the onions, top with mozzarella and scatter over the olives.

3 Bake in a preheated oven at 425°F for 15–20 minutes, until cooked and golden.

VARIATIONS

● Use standard onions in place of the red variety.

● Use chopped fresh oregano or marjoram in place of the chopped rosemary.

Tagliatelle with Pesto

THIS GREEN PESTO *is similar to the traditional Genoese version. It is best made in the summer, when basil has plenty of flavor.*

INGREDIENTS

⅔ cup basil leaves

½ cup pine nuts

7 tablespoons olive oil

2 garlic cloves, crushed

⅔ cup freshly grated
Parmesan cheese

salt and pepper

1 pound 2 ounces fresh tagliatelle

basil sprigs, to garnish

2 Add the Parmesan and seasoning and process briefly. Transfer to a small bowl, cover, and set aside.

TAGLIATELLE

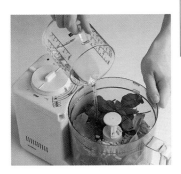

1 Process the basil leaves, pine nuts, olive oil, and garlic in a blender or small food processor until smooth.

3 Cook the pasta in a large saucepan of lightly salted, boiling water for about 3 minutes, or until just tender but still firm to the bite (*al dente*).

4 Drain the pasta thoroughly, return to the pan, add the pesto, and toss lightly to mix.

5 Garnish with fresh basil sprigs and serve the tagliatelle immediately.

VARIATION

Use pasta shapes such as fusilli (spirals) or conchiglie (shells) in place of tagliatelle.

Risotto with Asparagus and Fava Beans

SPECIAL RISOTTO RICE *is essential to get the correct creamy, moist consistency with rice grains that are slightly firm in the center.*

INGREDIENTS

6 shallots, finely chopped

2 garlic cloves, crushed

3 cups sliced mushrooms

2 celery stalks, finely chopped

1 tablespoon olive oil

generous 1 cup arborio (risotto) rice

1¼ cups dry white wine

2½ cups vegetable stock, kept simmering

salt and pepper

8 ounces fresh asparagus, cut into 1-inch lengths

1⅓ cups frozen baby fava beans

1 tablespoon chopped mixed herbs (optional)

fresh basil to garnish

Parmesan cheese shavings, to serve

Serves 4–6

BABY FAVA BEANS

1 Cook the shallots, garlic, mushrooms, and celery in the oil in a saucepan, stirring occasionally, for 5 minutes.

2 Add the rice and cook for 1 minute. Stir in the wine, bring to a gentle boil, and cook uncovered, over low heat, until the liquid has been absorbed, stirring frequently.

3 Continue adding stock, a ladleful at a time and stir frequently, until it has all been absorbed and the rice is creamy and tender, but still has a "bite." This will take about 25 minutes. Season.

4 Meanwhile, boil the asparagus for 6–8 minutes, until tender. Boil the fava beans for 3–4 minutes, until cooked. Drain both vegetables and keep warm.

Stir the vegetables, and herbs, if using, into the hot risotto and serve immediately, scattered with Parmesan shavings and garnished with basil. Serve with warm bread.

ASPARAGUS

VARIATIONS

- Replace shallots with onion.
- Substitute fresh green beans for the asparagus.
- Use fresh or frozen peas in place of fava beans.
- Use vegetable stock in place of the white wine.

Broiled Polenta with Mushrooms

CRISP BROILED POLENTA *served with succulent vegetables in a Marsala wine sauce makes a flavorsome and filling evening meal.*

INGREDIENTS

3 cups vegetable stock

salt and pepper, to season

1½ cups quick-cook or instant polenta

⅔ cup grated Parmesan cheese

1 tablespoon each chopped sage and rosemary

1 tablespoon olive oil, plus extra

1 small leek, finely chopped

2 garlic cloves, crushed

3 cups sliced exotic or large flat mushrooms

1½ cups quartered crimini mushrooms

2 tablespoons Marsala or dry sherry

2–3 tablespoons chopped flat leaf parsley

fresh herbs, to garnish

COOK'S TIP

Ready-prepared cooked polenta is available. Simply cut into strips and broil as directed.

1 Boil the stock and salt, add the polenta and cook until the mixture thickens and the stock is absorbed, stirring continuously. Simmer over a gentle heat for 10 minutes, stirring constantly.

2 Stir in the Parmesan, sage, rosemary, and pepper.

3 Spread the polenta on a damp cookie sheet in a rectangle about 1 inch thick. Leave in a cool place for about 1 hour, or until set.

4 Cut the polenta into 1-inch strips and brush lightly with oil. Broil on high heat for a few minutes on each side until lightly browned. Cover and keep warm.

VARIATIONS

● Add a few dried porcini (cep) mushrooms to the sautéed mushrooms, for extra flavor. Soak the dried mushrooms in warm water for about 20 minutes, drain, chop finely, and cook with the fresh mushrooms.

● Use 1 small onion in place of the leek.

5 Fry the leek and garlic in the olive oil for 3 minutes, stirring frequently. Stir in the mushrooms and cook for 3–4 minutes. Add the Marsala or sherry and cook over high heat, stirring, until some of the liquid has evaporated. Add the parsley and seasoning.

6 Serve the hot mushrooms and broiled polenta with a garnish of fresh herbs.

Spaghetti with Garlic and Chilies

THIS QUICK AND EASY *pasta dish is typical of southern Italy. Remove the seeds from the chilies for a milder flavor.*

INGREDIENTS

1 small onion, finely chopped

4 garlic cloves, finely chopped or crushed

2 fresh red chilies, finely chopped

6 tablespoons olive oil

1 pound 2 ounces fresh spaghetti

4 tablespoons chopped flat leaf parsley

flat leaf parsley sprigs, to garnish

freshly shaved Parmesan cheese, to serve

RED CHILIES

1 Cook the onion, garlic, and chilies in 1 tablespoon of oil in a skillet, stirring occasionally, for 5 minutes, or until the onion is softened but not browned.

VARIATIONS

● Use dried pasta instead of fresh. Allow 3–4 ounces per person. Cook for about 8–10 minutes.

● Use chopped fresh basil or oregano instead of parsley.

2 Meanwhile, cook the pasta in a large saucepan of lightly salted, boiling water for 3 minutes, or until just tender. Drain well.

3 Stir the garlic mixture into the remaining oil. Add the chopped parsley. Add the pasta to the mixture and toss together to mix well. Serve immediately, garnished with parsley and sprinkled with Parmesan shavings.

Vegetable Lasagne

A VEGETARIAN VERSION *of a classic Italian dish, this mixed vegetable lasagne is ideal for a family supper.*

INGREDIENTS

2 onions, sliced

2 garlic cloves, crushed

2 red bell peppers, seeded and sliced

1 yellow bell pepper, seeded and sliced

3 zucchini, sliced

3 cups sliced crimini mushrooms

14-ounce can chopped tomatoes

2 tablespoons sun-dried tomato paste

1 tablespoon chopped oregano

1 tablespoon chopped thyme

salt and pepper

5 tablespoons butter

9 tablespoons all-purpose flour

3¾ cups low-fat milk

1 teaspoon Dijon mustard

1 cup grated sharp Cheddar cheese

6 ounces fresh or no pre-cook lasagne sheets

½ cup freshly grated Parmesan cheese

Serves 4–6

VARIATIONS

● Use half-fat Cheddar cheese in place of standard Cheddar.

● An eggplant can be used instead of the zucchini.

● For added fiber use whole wheat lasagne.

ZUCCHINI

1 Cook the onions, garlic, bell peppers, zucchini, mushrooms, tomatoes, and tomato paste in a large, covered saucepan for 10 minutes, stirring occasionally. Add the herbs and seasoning, then set aside.

2 Gently heat the butter, flour, milk, and mustard in a saucepan, whisking until the sauce boils and thickens. Simmer gently for 3 minutes, stirring. Off the heat, stir in the Cheddar cheese and seasoning. Set aside.

3 Spoon half of the vegetables over the base of a shallow ovenproof dish and cover with half the lasagne. Top with one-third of the cheese sauce.

4 Repeat the layers, then finish with the remaining cheese sauce, covering the pasta completely. Sprinkle with Parmesan cheese. Bake in a preheated oven at 375°F for 40–45 minutes, or until golden and bubbling.

Sun-dried Tomato and Olive Focaccia

A DELICIOUS BREAD *made with readily available active dry yeast. Making bread dough is now reliable and very easy.*

INGREDIENTS

4 cups strong all-purpose white flour

2 teaspoons active dry yeast

1 teaspoon salt

2 ounces sun-dried tomatoes in oil, drained and chopped

½ cup pitted black olives, chopped

3 tablespoons olive oil, plus extra

1–1¼ cups tepid water

coarse sea salt, for sprinkling

Makes 1 focaccia (serves about 6)

1 Mix the flour, yeast, and salt together. Stir in the tomatoes and olives.

VARIATIONS

● Use half white and half whole wheat flour.

● Knead 2–3 tablespoons chopped fresh Italian herbs into the dough.

● Use mixed bell peppers in oil in place of the sun-dried tomatoes.

2 Make a well in the center, add 3 tablespoons oil and enough tepid water to make a soft, but not sticky dough.

3 Turn the dough onto a lightly floured surface and knead for 10 minutes, or until it is smooth and elastic.

4 Put in a bowl, cover with a clean dish cloth, and leave to rise until doubled in size.

5 Turn the dough onto a lightly floured surface and knead for 2–3 minutes. Roll out to a flat oval approximately 1 inch thick and place on a lightly greased cookie sheet.

6 Cover the dough with a dish cloth and leave until doubled in size again.

7 Use your fingers to make deep dents on the surface of the dough. Drizzle over a little oil and sprinkle with sea salt.

8 Bake in a preheated oven at 400°F for 20–25 minutes, or until cooked and golden.
Serve warm or cold, in slices or chunks, on its own or with a pasta, rice, or vegetable dish.

SUN-DRIED
TOMATOES

Tiramisu with Raspberries

THIS LIGHTER VERSION *of a popular Italian dessert combines low-fat yogurt with refreshing fruit and rich coffee liqueur.*

INGREDIENTS

2 eggs, separated

2 tablespoons superfine sugar

1 cup mascarpone cheese

1 cup low-fat natural yogurt

⅔ cup cold strong black coffee

7 tablespoons coffee liqueur
or brandy

18 sponge fingers; use savoiardi
if available

1⅓ cups fresh raspberries

sifted unsweetened cocoa , for sprinkling

Serves 6

CAUTION

This recipe contains raw eggs and should be avoided by more vulnerable or "at risk" groups, such as young children, pregnant women, the elderly or infirm, convalescents, or those who have an impaired immune system.

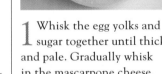

1 Whisk the egg yolks and sugar together until thick and pale. Gradually whisk in the mascarpone cheese, then fold in the yogurt until thoroughly blended.

2 In a separate bowl, whisk the egg whites until stiff.

Gently fold the whisked egg into the mascarpone mixture.

3 Mix the coffee and liqueur or brandy in a shallow dish. Dip 6 sponge fingers in this mixture for 10–15 seconds, so they become soaked, but not so soggy that they break.

4 Place the sponge fingers in the base of a glass serving dish. Scatter over ½ cup raspberries and spread one-third of the mascarpone mixture over the fruit.

5 Repeat these layers twice more. Sprinkle the top liberally with sifted unsweetened cocoa and chill for several hours or overnight.

Baked Ricotta Cheesecake

THIS DELICIOUS CHEESECAKE *can be served on its own or with fresh fruit, such as strawberries, raspberries, or peaches.*

INGREDIENTS

4 tablespoons butter, softened

4 tablespoons light brown sugar

¼ cup self-rising flour

¼ cup ground almonds

½ teaspoon baking powder

½ teaspoon ground cinnamon

4 eggs

2 cups ricotta cheese

6 tablespoons superfine sugar

finely grated rind and juice of 1 lemon

finely grated rind of 1 small orange

⅔ cup heavy cream

¼ cup all-purpose flour, sifted

¾ cup golden raisins

Serves 8–10

GRATED ORANGE RIND

1 Beat the butter, brown sugar, self-rising flour, almonds, baking powder, cinnamon, and 1 egg together until smooth. Spread the mixture evenly over the base of a greased and base-lined 8-inch round loose-based, deep cake pan.

2 Separate the remaining eggs. Process the egg yolks, ricotta cheese, superfine sugar, lemon rind and juice, orange rind, and cream in a blender or food processor.

3 Transfer to a bowl and fold in the flour and raisins.

VARIATIONS

● Use ground hazelnuts in place of almonds.

● Use chopped ready-to-eat dried apricots instead of golden raisins.

4 In a separate bowl, whisk the egg whites until stiff, then gently fold into the cheese mixture.

5 Pour into the pan and level the surface.

6 Bake in a preheated oven at 325°F for 1¼–1½ hours, or until just firm and golden. Let cool completely. Remove the cheesecake from the pan and place on a serving plate. Serve cold with fresh fruit or a little light cream.

Stuffed Peaches

FRESH FRUIT *is a popular way of rounding off an Italian meal. This recipe, which is very quick and easy to do, makes the fruit a little more special.*

INGREDIENTS

4 ripe peaches, halved, peeled, and pitted

3 tablespoons mascarpone cheese

3 tablespoons ricotta cheese

¼ teaspoon ground cinnamon

1 tablespoon superfine sugar

⅓ cup small fresh raspberries

toasted slivered almonds, to decorate

SLIVERED
ALMONDS

COOK'S TIP

If the peaches are difficult to peel, place them in a bowl, and cover with boiling water. Leave for about 30 seconds, then remove with a slotted spoon, and slip off the skins.

1 Put 2 peach halves, cut side up, on 4 serving plates.

2 Mix together the mascarpone cheese, ricotta cheese, cinnamon, and sugar in a bowl.

3 Fold the raspberries into the cheese mixture.

4 Pile the mixture into the peach half cavities, dividing it evenly among the peaches.
Sprinkle with slivered almonds to decorate and serve immediately.

VARIATIONS

● Use nectarines in place of the peaches.

● Crushed amaretti cookies or chopped nuts are a good alternative to almonds.

Lemon and Lime Sherbet

THIS REFRESHING SHERBET *is delicious served on its own or accompanied by fresh seasonal fruits.*

INGREDIENTS

1 cup sugar

2¼ cups water

finely grated rind and juice of 2 lemons

finely grated rind and juice of 2 limes

2 egg whites

pared lemon and lime rind, to decorate

Serves 4–6

VARIATIONS

● For a lemon sherbet use all lemons in place of limes.

● The rind and juice of 1 large orange can replace the limes.

1 Gently heat the sugar in a saucepan with the water, stirring until the sugar has dissolved, then boil for 3 minutes.

2 Off the heat, stir in the lemon and lime rinds and let cool. Stir in the fruit juices and then strain into a shallow plastic, freezerproof container.

Cover and freeze for about 2–3 hours, or until the mixture becomes slushy.

LIME HALVES

3 Turn into a chilled bowl and beat gently with a fork or whisk to break up the ice crystals.

CAUTION

This recipe contains raw eggs and should be avoided by more vulnerable or "at risk" groups, such as young children, pregnant women, the elderly or infirm, convalescents, or those who have an impaired immune system.

4 Whisk the egg whites until stiff. Fold them into the lemon mixture. Return to the container and freeze until firm.

Transfer to the refrigerator 30 minutes before serving in order to soften slightly. Serve decorated with pared lemon and lime rind.

Strawberries with Balsamic Vinegar

IT MAY SEEM *an unusual combination but the rich, sweet-sour flavor of balsamic vinegar really brings out the delicious flavor of the fruit.*

INGREDIENTS

4 cups ripe strawberries,
halved or sliced

2–3 tablespoons balsamic vinegar

superfine sugar, to taste

fresh mint sprigs, to decorate

1 Put the strawberries in a bowl and drizzle over the balsamic vinegar. Stir gently, then set aside for 15 minutes.

2 Sprinkle with sugar to taste and stir gently to mix. Decorate with fresh mint sprigs and serve immediately.

VARIATION

Use fresh lemon juice in place of balsamic vinegar.

Further reading

Antonio Carluccio, AN INVITATION TO ITALIAN COOKING (Pavilion Books Ltd, 1996)

Aldo Zilli, ALDO'S ITALIAN FOOD FOR FRIENDS (Metro Books, 1998)

Hilaire Walden, THE QUICK AFTER-WORK ITALIAN COOKBOOK (Piatkus Publishers Ltd, 1995)

Valentina Harris, RISOTTO! RISOTTO! (Cassell Plc, 1998)

Antonio Carluccio, PASSION FOR PASTA (BBC Books, 1996)

Elizabeth David, ITALIAN FOOD (Penguin Books, 1989)

Sarah Brown, FRESH VEGETARIAN COOKERY (BBC Books, 1995)

Anne Willan, PERFECT ITALIAN COUNTRY COOKING (Dorling Kindersley, 1997)

GOOD HOUSEKEEPING, STEP-BY-STEP VEGETARIAN COOKERY (Ebury Press, 1997)

Rose Elliot, VEGETARIAN COOKERY (Harper Collins, 1992)

Useful addresses

The Vegetarian Society
Parkdale
Durham Road
Altrincham
Cheshire WA14 4QG
UK

The Vegetarian Union of North America
PO Box 9710
Washington DC 20016
USA

The Australian Vegetarian Society
PO Box 65
2021 Paddington
Australia

The Soil Association
86 Colston Street
Bristol BS1 5BB
UK

Farm Verified Organic
RR 1
Box 40A USA
Medina
ND 58467
USA

National Association for Sustainable Agriculture
PO Box 768
AUS-Sterling
SA 5152
Australia